# YOUR KNOWLEDGE HAS VALUE

AF166859

- We will publish your bachelor's and master's thesis, essays and papers

- Your own eBook and book - sold worldwide in all relevant shops

- Earn money with each sale

## Upload your text at www.GRIN.com and publish for free

# The Influence of Leadership Attributes of the Principal on the Student's Academic Performance in Secondary Schools in Tanzania

## A Case of Mbulu District

Chelestino Mofuga

**Bibliographic information published by the German National Library:**

The German National Library lists this publication in the National Bibliography; detailed bibliographic data are available on the Internet at http://dnb.dnb.de.

ISBN: 9783346256317
This book is also available as an ebook.

© GRIN Publishing GmbH
Nymphenburger Straße 86
80636 München

Print and binding: Books on Demand GmbH, Norderstedt, Germany
Printed on acid-free paper from responsible sources.

The present work has been carefully prepared. Nevertheless, authors and publishers do not incur liability for the correctness of information, notes, links and advice as well as any printing errors.

GRIN web shop: https://www.grin.com/document/924973

# HOW LEADERSHIP ATTRIBUTES OF HEAD OF SCHOOLS INFLUENCES STUDENT'S ACADEMIC PERFORMANCE IN SECONDARY SCHOOLS IN TANZANIA: A CASE OF MBULU DISTRICT

*Author: Dr Chelestino Simbalimile Mofuga*

## ABSTRACT

This study assessed the influence of the leadership attributes of the Head of schools on the student academic performance in public and private secondary schools. Explanatory cross-sectional survey design with a concurrent mixed approach using both primary and secondary data were employed. A total of 202 teachers used to provide evidence on heads of schools attributes in influencing students' academic performance using questionnaires, in-depth interview and focus group discussion. The collected data were analysed using SPSS version 23 for quantitative data and thematic analysis for qualitative data. Significant relationship between integrity and students' academic performance was revealed. However, inspirational attributes negatively correlated between students' academic performance. In addition, the results reveal that there was weak, positive and significant relationship between competency and academic performance. The study concluded that integrity and competency attributes significantly influence positively the students' academic performance while inspirational negatively influences students' academic performance.

Therefore, the study recommends the government to allocate enough funds for professional development for the aspirant of head of secondary schools and review educational policy on the training and development of teachers before and after appointment into headship post.

**Key words**: leadership, leadership attributes Academic performance

**INDEX**

# ABBREVIATIONS

| | |
|---|---|
| HoS | Head of school |
| FGDs | Focused group discussion |
| SPSS | Statistical Package for Social Scientists |
| RCC | Regional consultative meetings |
| NECTA | National Examination Council of Tanzania |
| SD | Standard Deviation |
| SDA | Strongly Disagree |
| DA | Disagree |
| NT | Neither disagrees nor agrees |
| AG | Agree |
| SA | Strongly agree |

# 1. INTRODUCTION

The concept of leadership attributes in education context is of paramount for the education institutions like schools prosperity. The current study focused on head of school leadership attributes in influencing students' academic performance in secondary school. Leadership has a classical and vast history which associates many researchers work with it because there is an assumption that leaders are not born (Aline and Ramkumar, 2018), they can be developed (Darling-Hammond et al., 2007; Ardichvili, Dag, and Manderscheid, 2016). According to Northhouse (2007), leadership is a process of an individual to influence group(s) of individuals towards attainment of a common goal. Moreover, Swanson and Holton's (2001) defined leadership as application of expertise that is a combination of experiences, problem-solving skills, and knowledge in achieving a stipulated objective. Consequently, in the twenty-first century, a significance of leadership for successful operation of secondary schools had been widely acknowledged (Bennis and Naus, 2003).

Fundamentally, academics stand as a branch of education (Feather, 2016). While academics literally is knowledge especially on theoretical perspectives one gets by attending secondary school education, the later means inculcating the knowledge, moral values and positive thinking (Abubakar, 2018). According to Annie, Howard and Mildred (1996), academic performance is the outcome of education or the extent to which a student, teacher or institution has achieved their educational goals. Academic performance is measured by the final grade earned in the course. The Divisions are used as a convenient summary measure of the academic performance of secondary schools' students in Tanzania. The Divisions are better measurement because it provides a greater insight into the relative level of performance of individuals. Basically, various studies have applied such measurements in combination (Ismail, 2016). Traits theory of leadership identifies the specific personality traits that distinguish leaders from non-leaders. The theory focuses on the difference between leaders and followers assuming that leaders would display more personality traits than the subordinates (Cherry, 2106; Kanodia and Sacher, 2016). According to Cherry (2019), leadership traits are the consistent and habitual patterns of thoughts, feelings, behaviour, emotions or actions of the leader that distinguish the leader from the follower (Cherry, 2019). Leadership traits are not fixed but remain stable throughout a leader's life span.

Tomas Carlyle (1847) proposed the Great Man theory which relates with Traits Theory of leadership. Carlyle believed that "history is shaped by extraordinary leaders, and that the ability to lead was something they inherited at birth and not something that could be developed" (Spector, 2016; Pyke, 2018). Carlyle's theory of leadership was based on the rationale that people are "born" with leadership traits. Thus, most early researchers considered leaders traits to be permanent properties that were present at the birth of a future leader (Zaccaro, 2007). However, these views of leadership traits have evolved from several earlier perspectives of leadership. So, these ideas inspired researchers to look more into leadership and inheritable traits (Stogdill 1948; 1974; Zaccaro, 2001; 2007; Zaccaro et al., 2004; Yukl, 2006; Fleenor, 2006; Ricketts, 2009; Sage, 2011; Nichols and Cottrel, 2014; Pyke, 2018; Allens, 2018).

In earlier works there were no universal traits that predicted leadership in all situations. Leadership traits varied greatly. According to Zaccaro (2001), Zaccaro et al. (2004) and Yukl (2006), there are several integrated sets of leader attributes, including cognitive capacities, personality qualities, motives and values, problem solving skills and knowledge. Specifically, cognitive capacity includes general intelligence and creativity. Personality attributes includes adaptability, extroversion, risk taking, and openness. Motives and values include need for socialisation, achievement, and motivation. Problem solving skills include problem construction and solutions generation and self-regulation skills.

However, based on reviewed literature, this study identified three leadership attributes or traits; integrity, inspirational and competency, to assess influence of leadership attributes of head of schools on students' academic performance. As such, modern research on traits theory of leadership by Nichols and Cottrel (2014) provided the study with a wide-ranging leadership attribute which distinguishes leaders from followers, competence. A comprehensive leadership competence scale (LKS) was developed by Healthcare leader's alliance and the college of health care executives (2018) to measure competency attribute using 12 variables (appendix 1). There are several limitations with the trait theory. Limitations to trait theory would include identification of hundreds of different leadership traits. Thus, determining who is and isn't a successful leader solely based on traits has raised many different arguments, such as "What about great leaders who do not possess these traits," or "how come every person who exhibits these traits does not go on to become a great leader." With that being said, arguments and disagreements have been had as to what types of leadership traits are truly effective (Spector, 2016; Chery, 2016; 2019).

The charismatic leadership style was one of three leadership types described by Max Weber in 1947, along with the bureaucratic and traditional leadership styles (Epley, 2015). The charismatic leadership style is based on a form of heroism, almost of divine origin. According to Weber charisma separate ordinary people from great people and as the latter endowed with supernatural, superhuman or exceptional power (Sacavem et al., 2017), or as exemplary and on the basis of these extraordinary abilities the individual concerned is treated as a leader (Judge et al, 2006; Shamir, 2014; Antonakis, 2012). Moreover, there is an element of belief that charismatic leaders must inspire others to begin making progress toward their goals (Takala, 2005; Epley, 2015). A charismatic leader may have a forceful opinion, but they are also sensitive to the emotions, ambitions, and personal experiences that others have (Fairhurst and Uhl-Bien, 2012). These leaders recognize that it is the duty of the leader to adjust their approach to each person instead of forcing others to adjust themselves to their leadership style. Most importantly, a charismatic leader is willing to take a risk (Epley, 2015) and honest (Goolamaly and Ahmad, 2014). They recognize when it is necessary to be conservative and when a risk could bring in great rewards.

Therefore, a charismatic theory of leadership provided this study with integrity and inspirational attributes of leadership. As part of theoretical development, Bartholomew and Gustafson (1998) developed 30 variables to systematically measure integrity attribute while Francis and Barry (2004) developed 16 variables to analytically measure inspirational attribute. These variables were measured categorically in five-point scale (see Appendix 1). The theory did not furnish the study with competency attribute of leadership. According to the traits and charismatic theories of leadership, essential leaders' attributes are; self-confidence, integrity, dominance, charisma, ambitions, creativity, inspirational, motivation, competence, trustworthy and personal power. Moreover, Goolamaly and Ahmad (2014), identified and affirmed five major traits and charismatic leadership attributes: integrity, inspirational, competency, forward looking and self-efficacy. However, the, study selected only three wide-

6

ranging traits; integrity, inspirational and competence, because are universal leadership attributes (Antonnakis, 2012, Shamir, 2014, Duggar, 2015, Turknett, 2005, Quigley, 2007).

Although, trait and charismatic theories provided this study with integrity, inspirational and competency, the theories could not provide the criteria considered to promote a teacher into a school leadership position under the current decentralised education system in Tanzania. Hence, new public management theory was necessary. The new public management theory is the major approach employed by government to ensure ongoing educational reforms are effective. The NPM theory has emerged as the dominant one in educational governance. In the twenty $21^{st}$ century school leaders are supposed to have been working effectively to increase the performance of students academically. The effort to improve quality of education has been informed by Tanzania development vision 2025, MKUKUTA II (2012), Education and training policy (1995), and sub-sector plans. According to Mirunde, (2015), the study suggests that the head of schools lacks integrity, competency, and inspirational leadership attributes, as they are lacking training before and after appointment to sharpen their leadership attributes.

Likewise, Mbulu district has been struggling to improve school facilities to facilitate effective teaching and learning (RCC, Manyara Report, 2016) and the report shows that the district has surplus facilities and infrastructures for schools, compared to other districts in the country, yet the performance is poor, for instance, the NECTA results for 30 secondary schools from 2014 to 2018 were as follows: Division, I was 131, division II was 889, division III was 1684, division IV were 5012 and division 0 were 3087 students for just five years. Therefore, students got division four and zero 5012 and 3087 respectively are regarded as failures because they can't proceed with advanced level studies (NECTA, 2014, NECTA 2015, NECTA, 2016, NECTA, 2017 and NECTA, 2018). To accomplish this study focused into the following objectives:

## 2. OBJECTIVES OF THE STUDY

### 2.1 Main objective

To assess the influence of leadership attributes of Head of Schools on the student's academic performance in selected Secondary schools in Tanzania.

## 2.2 Specific objectives

In order to address the general objective, the study sought to accomplish the following four intertwined specific objectives:

i. To assess the influence of integrity attribute of Head of schools on the student academic performance in selected secondary schools.

ii. To assess the association between inspirational attributes of Head of schools on the students' academic performance in selected secondary schools.

iii. To assess the influence of competency attributes of Head of schools on the students' academic performance in selected secondary schools.

## 2.3 Empirical literature review

*Influence of integrity attributes of Head of schools on the student academic Performance in secondary schools*

Integrity is more than ethics at the individual level; it is all about the characters of the individual. It is those characteristics of an individual that are consistent, considerate, compassionate, transparent, honest, and ethical (Duggar, (2015). According to Turknett (2005), integrity is the foundation of the model and without integrity, no leader can be successful. Leaders with integrity will not twist facts for personal advantages, willing to stand up for and defending what is right, will be careful to keep promises; they counted on, to tell the truth. Integrity is the foundation of leadership and it involves a careful balance between respect and responsibility (Turknett, 2007). Lacking trust, competencies are meaningless. Individual who are not trustworthy will not be given opportunities or responsibilities and they will not be wanted as team members by clients or other employees (Quigley, 2007).

Furthermore, Goolamally and Ahmad, (2014) conducted a study in Malaysia to identify and affirm the conceptual framework and attributes of school leaders (principals) needed to achieve leadership sustainability and school excellence. The exploratory factor analysis method was employed for the purpose of this study. The research found that head of schools needs five attributes in order to excel in school leadership and make a school excellent:

8

integrity, inspirational, competency, forward-looking and self-efficacy. Thus, Integrity attribute, which has the sub-attributes of being principled and humble, was found to influence school achievement in Malaysia. This study focused on leadership attributes of the head of schools and ignored to assess the influence of attributes to student academic performance.

Therefore, based on the reviewed studies, there still inconclusive results of whether leadership attributes of head of school influences students' academic performance in secondary schools. Thus, there is no finding that has answered the question why secondary schools in Mbulu district are still performing poorly despite the effort by the government to employ qualified teachers, build more infrastructures, and provide appropriate textbooks, good salary and responsibility allowances (RCC, Manyara, 2016 and 2017 report.).

*Association of inspirational attributes of Head of schools and the student academic performance in secondary schools.*

Apolline (2015) examined the motivational strategies of principals in the management of selected secondary schools in Fako Division of the Southwest Region of Cameroon. The descriptive survey design was used to collect data from a representative sample of the population using questionnaires for teachers and principals. The data was analysed using means and standard deviation. The findings revealed that: motivational strategies of principals include those related to empathy or inspirational, supportive, caring and just on academic and disciplinary matter A study conducted by Goolamally and Ahmad, (2014) in Malaysia identified and affirmed the conceptual framework and attributes of school leaders (principals) needed to achieve leadership sustainability and school excellence. The study used quantitative research methods. The study found that head of schools needs five attributes in order to excel in school leadership and make a school excellent: integrity, inspirational, competency, forward-looking and self-efficacy. Thus, inspirational, which has the sub-attributes of supportive and influential, was found to influence school achievement in Malaysia. However, the study focused on leadership attributes of the head of schools and ignored to assess the influence of attributes to student academic performance, which is the focus of this study.

Mwangi (2011) conducted a study focusing on the effect of school leadership on student achievement in Kenya. The study employed both qualitative and quantitative in two distinct phases. In the first phase, the study used data obtained from 35 interviews with teachers and secondary school administrators, to gain an understanding of how leadership is enacted and experienced in daily school routines. The results showed that principal's engagement demonstrated inspirational, commitment, sensitivity to and focus on continuous improvement, and openness to information and diverse views, impacted student performance. In the final phase, the study used responses from 281 schools. The results indicated that school leadership had moderate but significant indirect effects on student achievement. A surprise finding was the negative impact of principals' advice and support on teachers' academic press.

Consequently, based on the reviewed studies, there still inconclusive results of whether inspirational attributes of head of school influences students' academic performance in secondary schools. Accordingly, to Wamala and Seruwagi (2013), a single leadership attribute alone may not directly translate into better students' academic performance. Thus, head of schools need to possess multitude of skills, competencies, cognitive abilities and person attributes which effective leaders possess.

### Competency attributes of Head of schools and the student academic performance in secondary schools.

Amuche and Saleh (2013) investigated the effectiveness and competency of principals of ECWA Secondary Schools in North Central Geo-political zone of Nigeria and how well they were professionally trained in School administration. It was also to find out how effective the training in-service was implemented in order to develop Principals and staff professional competency. Both qualitative and quantitative methods of research were employed in order to establish how competent the principals were in their leadership role. The study found out that most ECWA Secondary School principals, though educated in other fields, were not professionally competent in school administration and planning. Also, principals' managerial competence had a negative relationship (-0.02) with students' performance in ECWA secondary schools.

In addition, In addition, Goolamally and Ahmad, (2014) in their quantitative study identify and affirm the conceptual framework and attributes of school leaders (principals) needed to achieve leadership sustainability and school excellence in Malaysia, found that head of

10

schools needs five attributes in order to excel in school leadership and make a school excellent: integrity, inspirational, competency, forward-looking and self-efficacy. Thus, competent, which has the sub-attributes of task competency, action-oriented and sociability as well as emotional and spiritual competency, was found to influence school achievement in Malaysia. This study focused on leadership attributes of the head of schools and ignored to assess the influence of attributes to student academic performance.

Moreover, according to Robinson (2007), studies conducted on the qualitative research on the leadership attributes and the link to student outcomes were found to be only 24 published researches between 1985 to 2006 in Australia. Also, Mulford (2005), conducted a study to determine the contribution of leadership attributes on the student academic performance for five years between 2001 and 2005. The study found only 44 published academic journal articles. Thus, it can be postulated that there is inadequate research on the field of leadership attributes of head of schools and its influence on student academic performance today. Hence those studies show the empirical research gap of lacking of literature in leadership attributes and academic performance.

## 2.4 The Conceptual Framework

Theoretically, conceptual framework on attributes of school leaders towards achieving effective school leadership is based on the fact that the heads of schools are responsible for managerial and administration functions of managing, directing, planning, motivating and developing their staffs and students (Preetika and Priti, 2013). Traits and charismatic theories of leadership identified and affirmed the attributes of school leaders needed to achieve leadership sustainability and school excellence. The theories pointed out five all-inclusive important traits or attributes which a school leader or principal must possess in order to achieve better school and students' performance. These were; integrity, forward looking, inspirational, supportive and influential, and competent. However, the attributes of forward looking and supportive and influential were categorized as inspirational variables by Francis and Barry (2004) in their inspirational leadership measurement scale.

Competency refers to a high level of commitment and dedication, self-efficacy, emotional intelligence and the courage to take risks (Goolamaly and Ahmad, 2014). Thus, a competent

11

school leader has ability to monitor own feelings and emotions as well as those of other teachers (sensitivity, interpersonal skills), and to use this and available information to guide the schools' activities. This covers skills, behaviour, ability and knowledge to determine attitude, action, thought and communication style (Goleman, 1995). In addition, school leader's belief and confidence in his ability and skill to perform a task make a competent teacher effective in school leadership (Bandura, 1986). Theoretically, it was expected that the competence of school leaders would enhance the students' academic performance under their leadership.

**Independent variables    Intermediate variables    Dependent variable**

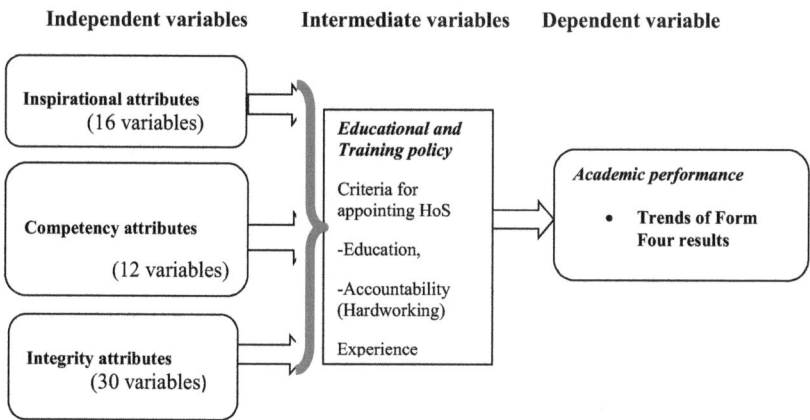

**Figure 2. 1:** Conceptual Framework of School Leaders' Attributes
**Source:** Theoretical and Empirical Literature Review

## 3. METHODOLOGY

To address the research objectives mixed research approach was opted. This allowed the use of explanatory and cross-sectional because it meticulously describes the influence of leadership attributes (integrity, inspirational and competency) on students' academic performance using data collected at one point in time. Thus, this design cannot gauge the temporal variations or a trend in the data collected (Kothari, 2009). Moreover, the survey design was selected because of its aptness in obtaining the obligatory quantity of data in running quantitative analysis as Hair *et al.*, (2006). A survey can also be standardized to allow an easy comparison of results (Nyamsogoro, 2010). The study compared the private and government schools, level of education offered, gender, education level and effect of training on academic performance of students.

Furthermore, the explanatory survey is an effective tool for getting a cause-effect relationship (Ghauri and Gronhaug, 2005) and the results can be generalized to a large population. As a result, the quantitative findings of this study were generalized to the whole Manyara region, and to the country, Tanzania. A total sample size of 237 was used, which was obtained using the formula developed by Yamane (1967), which was calculated as follows.

$$n = \frac{N}{1+N(\ell)^2} \dots\dots\dots\dots\dots\dots equation3.1$$

Where, $n=$ Sample size, $N=$ Population size with certain characteristics and $\ell=$ Precision factor coefficient $(5\%)$. This is also termed as the desired margin of error (ME) expressed as a proportion. According to Krejcie and Morgan (1970) and Tejada and Punzala (2012), this formula is simple and gives a high degree of accurate sample size, also fits with the available parameter N. Therefore, according to the formula:-

$$Sample(n) = \frac{583}{1+583x(0.05)^2} = 237 \dots\dots\dots\dots\dots equation3.2$$

$$n = 237$$

In this study, both quantitative and qualitative data were analyzed but separately. The aim was to draw valid inferences about what has been analysed and to avoid any spurious relationships. The quantitative data were subjected to computer software, Statistical Package for Social Science (SPSS) Version 23. Through the use of SPSS software, the researcher determined descriptive such as means, frequencies, and percentages as well as cross-tabulation or chi-square and model goodness of fit test between independent and dependent variables. In the course of presenting the findings, quantitative data were concretized by qualitative data obtained through interviews, focus groups, observations and information obtained from documents.

## 4. FINDINGS AND DISCUSSION

### 4.1 Influence of Integrity Attribute on the Students' Academic Performance

The results for first specific objective which aimed at assessing the influence of integrity attribute of the leadership of heads of schools on the students' academic performance in selected secondary schools in Mbulu district is presented in table 4.1 below. The results (Table 4.1) indicate that the item which says the head of school would steal from the organization scored the highest frequency of 85.70% (sum of 74.80% strongly disagreed and 10.90% disagreed). This means heads of schools cannot steal the school's resources. Therefore, the integrity attribute of trustworthy is possessed and practiced by heads of schools in Mbulu district. Accordingly, the second-highest score was found to be the item that says heads of schools can be trusted with confidential information (85.10%). So, heads of schools were found to be trustworthy in such a way that they cannot steal school's resources did not hurt someone's career because of a grudge (85.10%) nor they were hypocrite (85.10%).

Similarly, the item that asks if the head of schools would withhold information or constructive feedback because he/she wants someone to fail was the third important attribute of integrity with a frequency of 84.20%. Other items which scored highest frequencies and considered important attributes of integrity in Mbulu district include: would spread rumours or gossip to try to hurt people or the organization (84.20%), is rude or uncivil to co-workers (81.70%), shows unfair favouritisms toward some people (80.70%), would engage in sabotage of the organization (82.60%), likes to bend the rules (78.80%) and would make trouble for someone who got on his or her bad side (78.20%).

According to scholars such as Ojo (2011), Lumpkin, Claxton and Wilson (2014), Goolamally and Ahmad (2014) and Duggar, (2015), the HoS with the attribute of integrity are trustworthy,

14

sincere, transparent, just and, as much as possible, show congruence between their feelings, thoughts, actions and words. Besides, covers personal qualities such as self-respect, loyalty, and honesty towards oneself and staff and other stakeholders, do as they say, mentor their followers, have high moral values, not arrogant, not egoistic, courteous and respectful towards others. Thus, based on those qualities of effective secondary school leaders, in this study the 30 integrity constructs (items) were grouped into six categories of integrity attributes namely; trust, teamwork, sincere (not a hypocrite), altruistic (not selfish), not vindictive or arrogant and just (no favouritism).

**Table 4.1: Frequency Distribution of Integrity Indicators (N=202)**

| | Indicator | SDA N(%) | DA N(%) | NT N(%) | AG N(%) | SA N(%) |
|---|---|---|---|---|---|---|
| 1 | Puts personal interests ahead of organisation's | 109(54.00) | 29(14.40) | 17(08.40) | 36(17.80) | 11(05.40) |
| 2 | Would risk other people to protect himself or herself in works matters. | 117(57.90) | 26(12.90) | 19(09.40) | 35(17.30) | 05(02.50) |
| 3 | Enjoys turning down staffs requests | 92(45.50) | 30(14.90) | 32(15.80) | 31(15.30) | 17(08.40) |
| 4 | Deliberately fuels conflict between other people | 125(61.90) | 10(08.90) | 15(07.40) | 32(15.80) | 12(05.90) |
| 5 | Would blackmail an employee if she/he thought could get away with | 110(54.50) | 28(13.90) | 27(13.4) | 21(10.40) | 16(07.90) |
| 6 | Would deliberately exaggerate peoples mistake to make them look bad to others | 128(63.40) | 20(09.90) | 23(11.40) | 26(12.90) | 05(02.50) |
| 7 | Would treat some people better if they were of other sex or belonged to same ethnic group | 106(52.50) | 27(13.40) | 16(07.90) | 31(15.30) | 22(10.90) |
| 8 | Ridicules people for their mistakes | 43(21.30) | 18(08.90) | 18(08.90) | 58(28.70) | 64(31.70) |
| 9 | Can be trusted with confident information | 159(78.70) | 13(06.40) | 16(07.90) | 06(03.00) | 08(04.00) |
| 10 | Would lie to me | 101(50.00) | 31(15.30) | 34(16.80) | 25(12.40) | 11(05.40) |
| 11 | Is evil | 131(64.90) | 19(09.40) | 26(12.90) | 17(08.40) | 09(04.50) |
| 12 | Is not interested in task that don't bring him/her personal glory or recognition | 94(46.50) | 40(19.80) | 26(12.90) | 26(12.90) | 16(07.90) |
| 13 | Would violate organizational policy and then expect others to cover for him or her | 138(60.30) | 22(10.90) | 20(09.90) | 13(06.40) | 09(04.50) |
| 14 | Would allow someone else to be blamed for his or her mistake | 121(59.90) | 28(13.90) | 27(13.40) | 16(07.90) | 10(05.00) |
| 15 | Would deliberately not answer email, telephone /message to cause problems for someone else. | 122(60.40) | 32(15.80) | 15(07.40) | 18(08.90) | 15(07.40) |
| 16 | Would make trouble for someone who got on his or her bad side | 107(53.00) | 51(25.20) | 23(11.40) | 17(08.40) | 04(02.00) |
| 17 | Would engage in sabotage of the organization | 134(66.30) | 33(16.30) | 22(10.90) | 06(03.00) | 07(03.50) |
| 18 | Would deliberately distort what other people say | 120(59.40) | 33(16.30) | 21(10.40) | 23(11.40) | 05(02.50) |
| 19 | Is hypocrite | 154(76.20) | 18(08.90) | 16(07.90) | 09(04.50) | 05(02.50) |
| 20 | Is vindictive | 118(58.40) | 32(15.80) | 25(12.40) | 16(07.90) | 11(05.40) |
| 21 | Would try to take credit for other people's ideas | 71(35.10) | 46(22.80) | 30(14.90) | 39(19.30) | 16(07.90) |
| 22 | Likes to bend the rules | 131(64.90) | 28(13.90) | 19(09.40) | 15(07.40) | 09(04.50) |
| 23 | Would withhold information or constructive feedback because he/she wants someone to fail | 140(69.30) | 30(14.90) | 18(08.90) | 12(05.90) | 02(01.00) |
| 24 | Would spread rumours or gossip to try to hurt people or the organization | 146(72.30) | 24(11.90) | 18(08.90) | 07(03.50) | 07(03.50) |
| 25 | Is rude or uncivil to co workers | 131(64.90) | 34(16.80) | 21(10.40) | 11(05.40) | 05(02.50) |
| 26 | Would hurt someone's career because of grudge | 141(69.80) | 31(15.30) | 15(07.40) | 09(04.50) | 06(03.00) |
| 27 | Shows unfair favouritisms toward some people | 129(63.90) | 34(16.80) | 20(09.90) | 10(05.00) | 09(04.50) |
| 28 | Would steal from the organization | 151(74.80) | 22(10.90) | 12(05.90) | 13(06.40) | 04(02.00) |
| 29 | Would falsify records if it would help his/her work situation | 125(61.90) | 26(12.90) | 22(10.90) | 20(09.90) | 09(04.50) |
| 30 | Has a high moral standard | 34(16.80) | 12(05.90) | 25(12.40) | 56(27.70) | 75(37.10) |

**Source:** Field Data 2019

**4.2 Influence of Inspirational Attribute on the Student Academic Performance**

Accordingly, the results (Table 4.2) of the current study indicate that the item which says the head of school can manage others that will help them to do task scored the highest frequency of 79.20% (sum of 31.20% strongly disagreed and 48.00% disagreed). This means that the ability to manage others is the most important attribute of inspirational leadership in Mbulu district. Thus, the ability of heads of schools to mentor other teachers into effective and competent teachers is a key to improving the academic performance of students. Additionally, another highest score was found to be for the item that says heads of schools can lead organizational development process (79.20%). Needless to say, a good leader (HoS) is the one with outstanding leadership skills and can move the school forward through among others improving students' academic performance (Preetika and Priti, 2013; Evans *et al.*, 2016).

Also, measures of central tendency (mean and standard deviations) of every item for all participants and of all 16 items for every 202 participants were quantified to determine the distribution and variability of schools heads' inspirational attribute from the mean, on average (Table 4.2). The attribute of inspiration is a leadership characteristic which arouses the spirit of organization members to move forward, beyond what is expected or assigned. An inspirational HoS knows how to connect the self-concepts of the organization members to the leader's vision (Goolamally and Ahmad, 2014). Inspirational HoS use soft skills to capture the hearts of the organization members to work with full trust and confidence for the progress of the organization (Avery, 2004). Such a school leader stimulates the spirit of each individual to work hard for the organizational vision. Thus, when HoS get to know their teachers and students, they can motivate them to work for the success of the organization.

In a nutshell, the attribute of inspiration has two associate-attributes; motivator and influential (Goolamally and Ahmad, 2014). Motivator HoS is capable of building organization members' confidence in the work which needed to be done. Motivator HoS is clear about the work which needs to be performed, skilled in capturing the hearts of staff and students so that they continue striving and is courageous in facing changes. Meanwhile, influential HoS is skilled in pulling staffs and students to move forward together with them, encouraging them with motivating words so that they have initiative and never giving up in providing them with guidance.

17

**Table 4.2: Frequency Distribution of Inspirational Indicators (N=202)**

| | Indicator | SDA N(%) | DA N(%) | NT N(%) | AG N(%) | SA N(%) |
|---|---|---|---|---|---|---|
| 1 | Motivating other staff | 13(06.40) | 19(09.40) | 34(16.80) | 86(42.60) | 50(24.80) |
| 2 | Take role to run the organization | 03(01.50) | 14(06.90) | 31(15.30) | 94(46.50) | 60(29.70) |
| 3 | Take role to manage the system task exclusion | 09(04.50) | 14(06.90) | 49(24.30) | 84(41.60) | 46(22.80) |
| 4 | Directing the achievement of progress | 08(04.00) | 07(03.50) | 43(21.30) | 92(45.50) | 52(25.70) |
| 5 | Understand the need to change environment | 02(01.00) | 12(05.90) | 39(19.30) | 94(46.50) | 55(27.20) |
| 6 | Able to react appropriately to changes | 06(03.00) | 11(05.40) | 50(24.80) | 95(47.00) | 40(19.80) |
| 7 | Able to anticipate the risk that comes up from the decision-making process | 05(02.50) | 11(05.40) | 50(24.80) | 87(43.10) | 49(24.30) |
| 8 | Able to use current data to plan future success | 04(02.00) | 12(05.90) | 41(20.30) | 64(31.70) | 81(40.10) |
| 9 | Clear in ideas expressing | 07(03.50) | 08(04.00) | 35(17.30) | 91(45.00) | 61(30.20) |
| 10 | Able to encourage others | 04(02.00) | 10(05.00) | 30(14.90) | 80(39.60) | 78(38.60) |
| 11 | Able to relate with significance person from different organization | 04(02.00) | 08(04.00) | 41(20.30) | 95(47.00) | 54(26.70) |
| 12 | Take roles to solve the problems | 04(02.00) | 09(04.50) | 33(16.30) | 89(44.10) | 67(33.20) |
| 13 | Able to give guidance | 04(02.00) | 09(04.50) | 32(15.80) | 83(41.10) | 74(36.60) |
| 14 | Able to see the opportunity to succeed | 03(01.50) | 07(03.50) | 37(18.30) | 92(45.50) | 63(31.20) |
| 15 | Able to lead the organizational development process | 04(02.00) | 10(05.00) | 28(13.90) | 99(49.00) | 61(30.20) |
| 16 | Able to manage others that will help them to do the task | 04(02.00) | 08(04.00) | 30(14.90) | 97(48.00) | 63(31.20) |

**Source:** Field Data 2019

## 4.3 Influence of competency attribute on the student academic performance

The results on the influence of competency attribute of head of schools on the student academic performance in selected secondary schools in Mbulu district is indicated in table 4.3 below. The level of competency attribute of heads of schools in school leadership was measured by 11 statements or items of interest as indicated in Table 4.3. In order to answer the question, How to determine the competency attributes of the head of schools on the student academic performance in selected secondary schools in Mbulu district? Descriptive statistics such as frequency distribution and measures of central tendency (mean and standard deviations) of every item for all participants and of all 11 items for every 202 participants were quantified to measure the distribution and variability of school heads' competency attribute from the mean, on average.

Competency of the head of school is crucial as it defines what a leader does and how does it. For that reason, a school head must build school capacity through an effective leadership style to influence student achievement through teachers. To enable this school head must have or be able to develop the capacity and competency to work with school staffs to focus on curriculum, instruction and student learning outcomes.

The competency attribute has three sub-attributes, namely, work competency, emotional competency and spiritual competency (Goolamally and Ahmad, 2014). In one hand, items such as quality giving direction; ability to focus in the future; and professionalism fall under work competency. On the other hand, items Heads of schools being convincing when developing a vision; facilitation and negotiation; organizational climate and culture; and managing change are categorized as emotional competency. Also, contribution to the community and profession fall under spiritual competency.

**Table 4.3: Frequency Distribution of Competency Indicators (N=202)**

| | Indicator | SDA N(%) | DA N(%) | NT N(%) | AG N(%) | SA N(%) |
|---|---|---|---|---|---|---|
| 1 | Quality giving direction | 07(03.50) | 19(09.40) | 22(10.90) | 94(46.50) | 60(29.70) |
| 2 | Ability focusing on the future | 04(02.00) | 16(07.90) | 25(12.40) | 84(41.60) | 73(36.10) |
| 3 | Being convincing when developing a vision | 06(03.00) | 06(03.00) | 41(20.30) | 86(42.60) | 63(31.20) |
| 4 | Gripping vision be able to express values and strategies | 05(02.50) | 15(07.40) | 36(17.80) | 84(41.60) | 62(30.70) |
| 5 | Communication and relationship management | 03(01.50) | 12(05.90) | 32(15.80) | 78(38.60) | 77(38.10) |
| 6 | Facilitation and negotiation | 05(02.50) | 12(05.90) | 41(20.30) | 83(41.10) | 61(30.20) |
| 7 | Leadership skills and behaviour | 06(03.00) | 31(15.30) | 16(07.90) | 75(37.10) | 74(36.60) |
| 8 | Organization climate and culture | 04(02.00) | 09(04.50) | 45(22.30) | 108(53.50) | 36(17.80) |
| 9 | Managing change | 04(02.00) | 14(06.90) | 41(20.30) | 91(45.00) | 52(25.70) |
| 10 | Professionalism | 07(03.50) | 11(05.40) | 25(12.40) | 91(45.00) | 68(33.70) |
| 11 | Contribution to the community and profession | 06(03.00) | 08(04.00) | 29(14.40) | 93(46.00) | 66(32.70) |

**Source:** Field Data, 2019

But since the discrepancy is very small between the highest and the lowest (78.80%-70.70%=8.10%), this study implored that all attributes were very important items of competency. The items which scored lowest were; ability to manage change (70.70%), facilitation and negotiation skills (71.30%) and ability to manage organizational climate culture (71.30%). The HoS scored high in work and spiritual competence. Moreover, it was found in focus group discussion that HoS could manage schools, negotiate with client on-behalf of the school

19

community, and manages school activities as manager and facilitator. To consolidate this fact a teacher with a smile said that:

> *"The head of my school a good person, he had advised me to change my attitude*
> *to become a better teacher and person because he saw my potentials... I heeded*
> *his advice and now I have PhD, my students do not miss my class and I have*
> *impressive record based on pass marks on my subjects... with my PhD I don't feel*
> *like going to teach at university or college because I wish to be here"*

Consequently, the results of binary logistic regression model revealed that heads of schools without competency attribute of leadership were significantly less likely to report a pass in student academic performance compared to those with competency attribute (OR=0.052, $p<0.0000$). This means that the odds of having a pass in students' academic performance for heads of schools that were not competent was lower than (almost twenty times) that of heads of schools that were competent. Thus, in Mbulu district competency of heads of secondary schools influences students' academic performance positively. In other words, an increase in the competency of heads of schools in school leadership increases a pass grade of students'.

## 5. CONCLUSION

The study carried out to 202 teachers to provide evidence of the existence and application of integrity, inspirational and competency attributes among heads of schools and how those attributes influence student academic performance in Mbulu district. The findings of the study overwhelmingly support the assumptions that, integrity, inspirational and competency attributes significantly influence students' academic performance. However, the direction of no integrity and no competency were negative while no inspirational was positive. It is recommended that induction and in-service training on leadership behaviour, management skills, instructional leadership and professional development for the newly appointed heads of school to equip the immature heads in their administrative and management duties are of paramount as it reinforces leadership attributes.

## 6. REFERENCES

Aaker, D.A., Kumar, V., and Day, G.S. (2001). *Marketing research*. New York, USA: John Wiley and Sons Inc. Page 751

Abubakar, U. (2018). The difference between education and academics (Blog post). Accessed from https://tutors.com.ng/2018/08/02/the-difference-between-education-and-academics/html

Ache Health Care. (2018). *Health care leader's alliance and the college of healthy executives' competencies assessment tool*. USA. Author.

Adam, J. and Kamuzora, F. (2008). *Research methods for business and social studies*. Morogoro, Tanzania: Mzumbe Book Project.

Adebayo, F.A. (2009). Parents' preference for private secondary schools in Nigeria. Kamla-Raj 2009. *International Journal of Education Science, 1(1), 1-6*

Adeleye, J.O. (2017). Pragmatism and its implications on teaching and learning in Nigerian schools. *Research Highlights in Education and Science*, Page 2-6

Adeyemi, O. T. (2013). Principal's leadership styles and student academic performance in secondary schools in Ekiti State, Nigeria. *International Journal of Academic Research in Progressive Education and Development*. 2(1), 187-198

Afeli, (2017). *Regional workshop on national learning assessment systems in Sub-Saharan Africa: Knowledge sharing and needs assessment*. Paper presented at the UNESCO and TALENT Workshop on National Learning Assessment Systems in Dakar, Senegal from 6th to 8th December, 2017.

Ahmed, J.U. (2010). Documentary research method: New dimensions. *Indus Journal of Management and Social Sciences*, 4(1), 1-14

Ahmed, S. (2009). Statistical methods for sample surveys (140.640): Introduction to sampling method (Lecture). University of John Hopkins.

Ahmet, AVCI. (2016). Effect of leadership styles of school principals on organizational citizenship behaviours. *Educational Research and Reviews*, 11(11), 1008-1024

Ajayi, V.O. (2017). *Primary sources of data and secondary sources of data; Distinguish between primary sources of data and secondary sources of data*. Benue State University, Makurdi. Faculty of Education Department of Curriculum And Teaching

Akaranga, S.I. and Makau, B.K. (2016). Ethical considerations and their applications to research: a Case of the University of Nairobi. *Journal of Educational Policy and Entrepreneurial Research, 3(12), 1-91.*

Akiri, (2017). Lecturer's professional competency and student academic performance, in Indonesia Higher Education. *International Journal of Human Resources Studies*, 7 (1).

Akiri, A.A. (2013). Effects of teachers' effectiveness on students' academic performance in public secondary schools; Delta State – Nigeria. *Journal of Educational and Social Research*, 3(3)

Aline, I. and Ramkumar, S. (2018). Leaders are not born, they are made. *International Journal of Applied Research*, 4(5), 94-96

Al-Karasneh, S. and Jubran, A. (2013). Classroom leadership and creativity: A study of social studies and islamic education teachers in Jordan. *Creative Education*, 4(10)

Alkarni, A. (2015). Problems which may challenge the ability of secondary school head teachers in the City of Tabuk to lead their schools professionally. *ARECLS*, 11, 55-74.

Allen, N., Grigsby, B. and Peters, M.L. (2015). Does leadership matter? Examining the relationship among transformational leadership, school climate, and student achievement. *NCPEA International Journal of Educational Leadership Preparation*, 10(2)

Allport, G. W., and Odbert, H. S. (1936). Trait names. A psycho-lexical study. *Psychological monographs*, 47, pp 211.

Almalki, S. (2016). Integrating quantitative and qualitative data in mixed methods research—challenges and benefits. *Journal of Education and Learning*; 5(3)

Al-Saleh, M.F. and Yousif, A.E. (2009). Properties of the Standard Deviation that are rarely mentioned in classrooms. *Austrian Journal of Statistics*, 38(3), 193–202

Alvaro, C., and Maria, G. (2017). *Does school leadership affect student academic achievement?* Fundació Jaume Bofill, Ivàlua.

Amuche, C.I. and Saleh, D.A. (2013). Principals managerial competence asa correlate of students' academic performance in Ecwa secondary schools in North Central Nigeria. *Journal of Education and Practice*, 4(4).

Annie, W., Howard, W.S. and Mildred, M. (1996). Achievement and ability tests: Definition of the domain. Educational Measurement 2, University Press of America, pages 2–5.

Appoline, A.T. (2015). *Motivational strategies used by principals in the management of schools. The Case of some selected secondary schools in the Fako division of the Southwest region of Cameroon.* Master's Thesis in Education, Department of Education, University of Jyvaskyla.

Ardichvili, A., Dag, K.N. and Manderscheid, S. (2016). Leadership development: Current and emerging models and practices. *Advances in Developing Human Resources*, 18(3), 275-285.

Arshad M., Zaidi, S.M.I.H and Mahmood K. (2015). Self-Esteem and academic performance among university students. *Journal of Education and Practice*, 6(1), 156-162

Asimaki A., and Vergidis K. D. (2013). Detecting the gender dimension of the choice of the teaching profession prior to the economic crisis and imf (international monetary fund) memorandum in Greece: A case study. *International Educational Studies*, 6(4), 140–153.

Avery, G.C. (2004) *Understanding leadership: Paradigms and cases*. London: Sage.

Awiti, F. S. (2013). *Management strategies of teachers turn over in Ilala municipal*. A Dissertation Submitted for Partial Fulfilment of the Requirements for the Award of the Degree of Masters of Science in Human Resources Management of Mzumbe University.

Ayeni, A. J. (2005). *The effect of principals' leadership styles on motivation of teachers for job performance in secondary schools in Akure South local government*. A Dissertation Submitted to the Department of Educational Administration and Planning for Partial Fulfilment of Award of Masters Art in Education of Obafemi Awolowo University, Ile-Ife.

Azaliwa, E.A and Casmir, A. (2016). A comparative study of teachers' motivation on work performance in selected public and private secondary schools in Kilimanjaro region, Tanzania. *International Journal of Education and Research. 4(6)*, 583-600

Babajani, J. (2008). The analysis theatrical and legal basis of 2008 budgeting new approach of view accountability, *Hesabdar*, 194, 4-5

Babajani, J. (2010). Challenges of public sector financial reporting. *Hesabras*, 48, 96-97

Bahta, S.T. and Bauer, S. (2007). *Analysis of the determinants of market participation within the South African small-scale livestock sector*. Tropentag, October 9 -11, 2007, Witzenhausen: Utilisation of diversity in land use systems: Sustainable and organic approaches to meet human needs. Tropentag Paper.

Bailey, K.D. (1982). *Methods of social research* (2nd Ed.). New York: Free Press. 553 p

Balihar, S. (2007). Qualitative research methods: documentary research (Blog post). Accessed from http://uk.geocities.com/balihar_sanghera/qrmdocumentaryresearch.html

Balliro, M.J. (2018). *The new sincerity in American literature.* A dissertation submitted in partial fulfilment of the requirements for the Degree of Doctor of Philosophy in English of University of Rhode Island

Bandura, A. (1997). *Self-efficacy: The exercise of control.* New York: W.H Freeman and Company

Baron, R.M., and d Kenny, D.A. (1986). The moderator–mediator variable distinction in social psychological research: Conceptual, strategic, and statistical considerations. *Journal of Personality and Social Psychology,* Volume 51(6), 1173–1182

Barth, R.S. (2009). *Improve schools from within: Teachers, parents, and principles can make a difference.* San Francisco, CA: Jossey-Bas.

Bass B. M., (1990). *Bass and Stogdills handbook of leadership. theory research and managerial application.* New York: Free Press.

Baum, D.R. and Riley, I. (2018). The relative effectiveness of private and public schools: evidence from Kenya. *An International Journal of Research, Policy and Practice.*

Baxter, and Jack, (2008). Qualitative case study methodology: Study design and implementation for novice researchers. *The Qualitative Report,* 1(4), 554-559.

Bedi, A. S., and Garg, A. (2000). The Effectiveness of private versus public schools: The C\case of Indonesia. *Journal of Development Economics,* 61(2), 463-494.

Begna, T.N. (2017). Public schools and private schools in Ethiopia: Partners in national development? *International Journal of Humanities Social Sciences and Education, 4(2), 100-111*

Bennel, P. and Mukyanuzi, F. (2005). *Is there a teacher motivation crisis in Tanzania?* Research Report Fund. Dar es Salaam: HR-Consult.

Bennell, P. (2004). *Teacher motivation and incentives in Sub -Saharan Africa and Asia.* Brighton: Knowledge and Skills for Development

Bennis, W. G., and Naus, B. (2003). *Leaders: The strategies for taking charge.* New York: Harper and Row.

Bernardo, A. B. I., Ganotice, F.A. and King, R.B. (2014). Motivation gap and achievement gap between public and private high schools in the Philippines. *The Asia-Pacific Education Researcher,* 24(4).

Bill, M. (2008). *The leadership challenge in improving learning in schools.* Australia: Australia Council for Educational Research,

Black, P.J., Woodworth, M. and Porter, S. (2014). The big bad wolf? The relation between the dark triad and the interpersonal assessment of vulnerability. *Personality and Individual Differences,* 67, 52-56.

Blanche, M. T., Durrheim, K. and Painter, D. (2006). *Research in practice: Applied methods for the social sciences.* Juta and Company Ltd.

Bleiklie, I. and Michelsen, S. (2013). Comparing higher education policies in Europe: Structures and reform outputs in eight countries', *Higher Education,* 65, 113–133.

Bleiklie, I., Enders, J., Lepori, B. and C. Musselin (2011). New public management, network governance and the university as a changing professional organization', in T. Christensen and P. Laegreid (eds) *The Ashgate Research Companion to New Public Management,* (pp. 161–176) (Farnham: Ashgate).

Bloor, M., Frankland, J., Thomas, M., and Robson, K. (2001). *Focus groups in social research.* London, Thousand Oaks -CA: Sage Publications Inc.

Bolat O.İ, Bolat T, and Seymen O.A (2009). Güçlendirici lider davranışları ve örgütsel vatandaşlık davranışı arasındaki ilişkinin sosyal mübadele kuramından hareketle incelenmesi. Balıkesir Üniversitesi Sosyal Bilimler Enstitüsü Dergisi 12(21), 215-239.

Boniface, R., (2016). *Teachers' retention in Tanzanian remote secondary schools: Exploring perceived challenges and support.* Doctoral dissertation, Department of Education, Linnaeus University, Sweden.

Bowen, G. A. (2009). Document analysis as a qualitative research method. *Qualitative Research Journal,* 9(2), 27-40. doi:10.3316/QRJ0902027

Braun, V. and Clarke, V. (2006) Using thematic analysis in psychology. *Qualitative Research in Psychology,* 3 (2), 77-101.

Burns, N., and Grove, S. K. (2003). *The practice of Nursing Research: Conduct, critique and utilization.* Philadelphia: W. Saunders.

Byabato,S., and Kisamo, K. (2014). Implementation of school based continuous assessment in Tanzania ordinary secondary schools and its implications on the quality of education. *Developing Country Studies,* 4(6)

Campanelli, P. (2008). Testing survey questions. In E.D. De Leeuw, J.J. Hox, and D.A. Dillman (Eds), *International Handbook of Survey Methodology,* New York: Lawrence Erlbaum Associates

Cardoso, S., Carvalho, T. and Santiago, R. (2011). From students to consumers: Reflections on the marketisation of Portuguese higher education', *European Journal of Education*, 46(2), 271-284.

Caspar, R., Peytcheva, E., Yan, Y., Lee, S., Liu, M. and Hu, M. (2016). Pretesting Cross-cultural survey guidelines. CC56

Ceil, C., and Sykes, J. (2012). *Women in leadership*. New York: Social Science Electronic Publishing Inc. Retrieved November 28, 2015, from http://ssrn.com/abstract=2051415

Cerit, Y. (2009). The effects of servant leadership behaviours of school principals on teachers' job satisfaction. *Educational Management Administration and Leadership* 37(5), 600–623

Gbollie, C. and Keamu, H.P. (2017). Student academic performance: The role of motivation, strategies, and perceived factors hindering Liberian junior and senior high school students learning. *Education Research International*, Volume 2017, Article ID 1789084, 11 pages

Chaudhary, A.K. and Israel, G.D. (2014). The Savvy survey #8: Pilot testing and pretesting questionnaires. IFAS extension, University of Florida

Cheng, Y.C and Townsend, T. (2000). Educational change and development in the Asian Pacific region: trends and issues, In T. Townsend and Y.C. Cheng (Eds). *Educational change and development in the Asia-Pacific region: Challenges for the future,* Rotterdam: Swets and Zeitlinger.

Cherrington, David J. and J. Owen, Cherrington (1993). Understanding honesty. *Internal Auditor, pp* 29-35.

Cherry, K. (2016). *What is the trait theory of leadership?* Retrieved from https://www.verywell.com/what-is-the-trait-theory-of-leadership-2795322

Cherry, K. (2019). *How extroversion in personality influences behaviour.* Accessed from https://www.verywellmind.com/what-is-extroversion-2795994

Cho, J., and Trent, A. (2006). Validity in qualitative research revisited. *Qualitative Research,* 6(3), 319-340.

Chrzanowska, J. (2002). *Interviewing groups and individuals in qualitative market research* (Vol. 2). London: Sage. 176 p

Churchil, G.A. and Iacobucci, D. (2005). Marketing research: Methodological foundation (9th Ed.). USA: Thomson South-Western

Churchill, G. A. (1996). *Basic marketing research (3rd Ed.),* Fort Worth, TX: The Dryden Press

Clarke, J., and Wood, D. (2001). New public management and development: The case of public service reform in Tanzania and Uganda. In McCourt, W., and Minongue, M., (Eds.), *the Internationalization of public management: Reinventing the Third World State.* Cheltenham, Edward Elgar.

Clarke, V., and Braun, V. (2013). Teaching thematic analysis: Overcoming challenges and developing strategies for effective learning. *Psychologist, 26*(2), 120-123.

Cohen, L., Manion, L., and Marrison, K. (2007). *Research methods in education (6th edition).* London: Routledge Taylor and Francis group. 638 p.

Conger J.A., and Kanungo R.N, (1987). Charismatic leadership in organization perceived behavioural –attributes and their measurement. *A Journal of Organizational Behavioural,* 15, 439-452.

Conroy, R.M. (2016). The RCSI sample size handbook: A rough guide

Cortina, J.M. (1993). What is coefficient Alpha? An examination of theory and applications. *Journal of Applied Psychology,* 78(1), 98-104

Creswell, J. W. (2007). *Qualitative inquiry and research design: Choosing among five approaches (2nd ed.).* Thousand Oaks, CA, US: Sage

Creswell, J. W. (2014). *Research design: Qualitative, quantitative, and mixed methods approaches.* Sage. 342 p.

Creswell, J. W., and Plano Clark, V. L. (2011). *Designing and conducting mixed methods research* (2nd ed.). London: Sage.

Creswell, J. W., Fetters, M. D. and Ivankova, N. V. (2004). Designing a Mixed methods study in primary care. *The Annals of Family Medicine, 2*(1), 7-12.

Creswell, J.W. (2009) *Research design: qualitative, quantitative, and mixed methods approaches* (3rd Ed.). Thousand Oaks, CA: Sage.

Crossman, A., and Harris, P. (2006). Job satisfaction of secondary school teachers. *Educational Management and Leadership, 34(1),* 29-46.

Crow, G. (2001). School leader preparation: A short review of the knowledge base. National College for School Leadership. Available at http://www.ncsl.org.uk/mediastore/image2/randd-gary-crow-paper.pdf

Cuthill, M. (2002). Exploratory research: citizen participation, local government and sustainable development in Australia. *Sustainable Development,* 10, 79-89.

Dang, V. H. (2015). A mixed method approach enabling the triangulation technique: A case study in Vietnam. *World Journal of Social Science*, (2)2

Daniel, R. (2003). *The Role of school leadership on student achievement.* Luxemburg, Italy.

# YOUR KNOWLEDGE HAS VALUE

- We will publish your bachelor's and
  master's thesis, essays and papers

- Your own eBook and book -
  sold worldwide in all relevant shops

- Earn money with each sale

Upload your text at www.GRIN.com
and publish for free